Be radiant

FROM THE INSIDE OUT.

July 1

D0150835

You
ARE
God's sweet
beautiful CREATION
& He loves you
with ALL His heart.

June 30

A happy face means a glad heart.

PROVERBS 15:13 TLB

July 2

I have loved you
with an everlasting love.

JEREMIAH 31:3 NKJV

The Lord make His face
shine on you,
and be gracious to you.

NUMBERS 6:25 NASB

July 3

Charm is deceptive,
and beauty is passing,
but a woman who fears the Lord,
she shall be praised.

PROVERBS 31:30 NKJV

June 28

Let the peace of Christ rule in your hearts.

COLOSSIANS 3:15 NRSV

DATE

_____

FROM

_____

PRESENTED TO

His grace shines ON MY FACE AND THAT makes me beautiful.

Pursue inner beauty.

Therefore I take pleasure
in infirmities...for Christ's sake.
For when I am weak,
then I am strong.

II CORINTHIANS 12:10 NKJV

July 5

YOU WERE CREATED IN THE *glorious image* OF GOD.

God created man
in His own image...
male and female
He created them.

GENESIS 1:27 NASB

MAY THE GOD OF HOPE
FILL YOU WITH ALL JOY
AND PEACE IN BELIEVING.

ROMANS 15:13 NRSV

He will take delight
in you with gladness.
With His love,
He will calm all your fears.
He will rejoice over you
with joyful songs.

ZEPHANIAH 3:17 NLT

June 24

Lord, You are our Father; we are the clay, and You our potter; and all we are the work of Your hand.

ISAIAH 64:8 NKJV

July 8

You are
ENJOYED, VALUED, & LOVED
just because you're YOU!

June 23

Put on comfortable shoes and head in the direction of your dreams—God has prepared the path ahead of you.

FOR WE KNOW,
BROTHERS AND SISTERS
BELOVED BY GOD,
THAT HE HAS CHOSEN YOU.

I THESSALONIANS 1:4 NRSV

You can do *great things* if you focus on the *great God* who created you!

God has chosen

you...

His treasured possession.

DEUTERONOMY 7:6 NRSV

Be strong and bold...because it is
the Lord your God who goes with you;
He will not fail you or forsake you.

DEUTERONOMY 31:6 NRSV

July 11

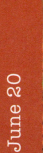

June 20

YOU ARE GOD'S

beautiful treasure

joy is one of the best accessories.

WE ARE GOD'S
masterpiece.

EPHESIANS 2:10 NLT

June 19

The people who know their God

shall be strong and do

great things.

DANIEL 11:32 TLB

July 13

WONDERFULLY

made

AND

COMPLETELY

loved.

These trials are only
to test your faith,
to see whether or not
it is strong and pure.

I PETER 1:7 TLB

The beauty around you
is nothing compared to
God's beauty within you.

God's word renews the spirit, soul, and body.

July 15

THE HEAVENS DECLARE *the Glory of God* THE SKIES PROCLAIM THE *work of His hands.*

PSALM 19:1 NIV

Make the most   of the opportunities

God gives you   to shine today.

The Lord designed every detail of who you are.

THE

joy

OF THE LORD IS

YOUR STRENGTH.

NEHEMIAH 8:10 NKJV

You formed...me in my mother's womb.

PSALM 139:13 NKJV

CALENDARS ARE
GOOD FOR
ORGANIZING DAYS...
BUT ONLY GOD
CAN ORGANIZE LIFE.

You [are] precious in My sight,
You have been honored,
and I have loved you.

ISAIAH 43:4 NKJV

LORD, LEAD THE WAY.

July 19

God's love is the only mirror that can reflect your *true beauty.*

June 12

I have learned the secret of living in every situation.

PHILIPPIANS 4:12 NLT

July 20

God chose you.

II THESSALONIANS 2:13 NRSV

June 11

Step out the door

each day

with a heart

full of *courage*.

You are valued and loved

just because

God made you!

TRUST SHOULD BE IN GOD, WHO RICHLY GIVES US *all we need* FOR OUR ENJOYMENT.

1 TIMOTHY 6:17 NLT

July 22

The imperishable quality
of a gentle and quiet spirit…
is precious in the sight of God.

I PETER 3:4 NASB

You, O Lord,
are a shield for me,
my glory and the One
who lifts up my head.

PSALM 3:3 NKJV

God's beauty is found in
His heart...
my beauty is found in
HIM.

June 8

Love

NEVER GOES OUT

OF STYLE.

July 24

June 7

God looked over all He had made, and He saw that it was very good!

GENESIS 1:31 NLT

Believe you can change the world and God will show you how.

You are a special person created by an awesome God.

YOU CAN GET ANYTHING—
ANYTHING YOU ASK FOR
IN PRAYER—IF YOU BELIEVE.

MATTHEW 21:22 TLB

I love You,
O LORD.

PSALM 18:1 NASB

There is radiance in a woman who knows how priceless she is to God.

THE DEFINITION
— of —
Lovely
IS BEING IN LOVE
with God.

June 4

Let love guide your life.

COLOSSIANS 3:14 TLB

July 28

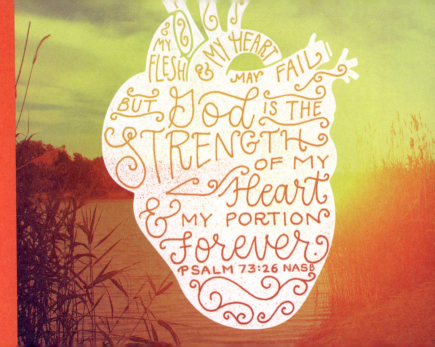

MY FLESH & MY HEART MAY FAIL BUT GOD IS THE STRENGTH OF MY Heart & MY PORTION Forever
PSALM 73:26 NASB

June 3

Happy are those
who are strong in the Lord,
who want above all else
to follow Your steps.

PSALM 84:5 TLB

*True and lasting beauty is this—
the reflection of God's heart in
and through you.*

June 2

If you can

pray,

you can

conquer!

*What matters
is what's
on the inside.*

Take courage...
your sins
are forgiven.

MATTHEW 9:2 NASB

July 31

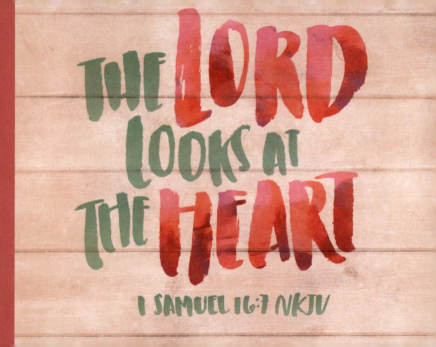

THE LORD LOOKS AT THE HEART

1 SAMUEL 16:7 NKJV

God created
every soul to
sing!

He has MADE
EVERYTHING
beautiful
IN ITS TIME.
ECCLESIASTES 3:11 NKJV

May 30

A person needs little else
besides prayer
to get through the day.

Everything beautiful

BEGINS WITH GOD.

Your greatest glory will be that
you belong to Him.

II THESSALONIANS 1:12 TLB

God's joy is your strength,

and His love is your shield.

You've got what it takes

to be amazing!

You are a *child of God.*

August 4

be strong through the grace God gives you

May 27

LOOK UP AND KNOW THAT EVERYTHING WILL BE MORE THAN OK— IT WILL ALL WORK OUT *perfectly.*

Therefore, if anyone is in Christ, he is a new creation. The old has passed away... the new has come.

2 CORINTHIANS 5:17 ESV

May 26

If two of you agree down here on earth concerning anything you ask for, my Father in heaven will do it for you.

MATTHEW 18:19 TLB

God is a changer.

He changes deserts...
        into places of rain.

He brings the oppressed...
        hope and life again.

He takes the old...
        and makes it new.

He turns your sorrows...
        into joys for you.

Pay all your debts except the debt of love for others—never finish paying that!

ROMANS 13:8 TLB

God meets you

where you are

&

takes you

where you need to go.

IT'S ALL ABOUT

Love

August 8

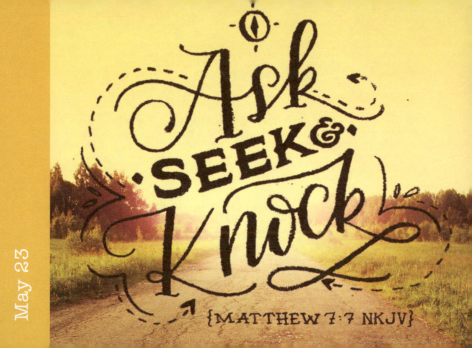

The Lord will give you an abundance of good things.

DEUTERONOMY 28:11 TLB

August 9

God cares about every detail of your life.

A cheerful heart

does good like medicine.

PROVERBS 17:22 TLB

Are not two sparrows sold for a penny?
Yet not one of them will fall to the ground
apart from your Father. And even the hairs
of your head are all counted.
So do not be afraid; you are of more value
than many sparrows.

MATTHEW 10:29–31 NRSV

May 21

Wisdom in three words:

Holy Spirit, come!

Oh, worship the LORD

in the beauty of holiness!

PSALM 96:9 NKJV

Love the Lord your God with all your heart, soul, and mind.

MATTHEW 22:37 TLB

August 12

May 19

Life is *Beautiful* because God is beautiful.

With God

all things

are possible.

MARK 10:27 NKJV

NOTHING CAN SEPARATE YOU FROM GOD'S OVERFLOWING *Love*

May 18

God is working on your behalf
this very moment.

For I am convinced that
neither death, nor life,
nor angels, nor principalities,
nor things present, nor things to come,
nor powers, nor height, nor depth,
nor any other created thing,
will be able to separate us
from the love of God,
which is in Christ Jesus our Lord.

ROMANS 8:38–39 NASB

Sit quietly.
Breathe deeply.
Hope steadily.

Delighting in God
is His invitation
to know Him and His love.

Turn to God....
Then times of refreshment
will come from the
presence of the Lord.

ACTS 3:19–20 NLT

May 15

Delight yourself in the Lord

PSALM 37:4 ESV

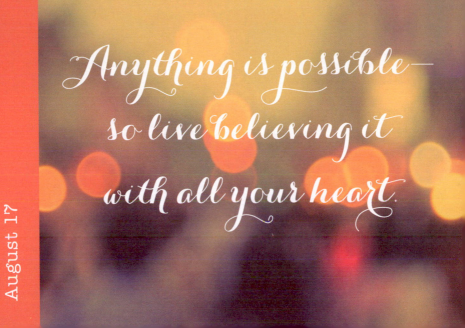

Anything is possible—
so live believing it
with all your heart.

August 17

GOD HAS
CALLED YOU
TO AN
INCREDIBLE
PURPOSE,
AND HE
BELIEVES
IN YOU.

May 14

Be good
to yourself.
God only made
one of you!

FOR IT IS

GOD

WHO IS AT WORK IN YOU,
ENABLING YOU BOTH
TO WILL AND TO WORK
FOR HIS GOOD PLEASURE.

PHILIPPIANS 2:13 NRSV

There will be bumps
in the road,
so hold onto
God's promises
with both hands.

The secret
to peace and rest
lies in God's
complete faithfulness.

I refresh the humble and give new courage to those with repentant hearts.

ISAIAH 57:15 TLB

August 20

He Is *Faithful*

1 John 1:9 NKJV

May 11

THOSE WHO WAIT

FOR THE LORD,

THEY WILL

inherit

THE LAND.

PSALM 37:9 NASB

May 10

For the **LORD** is good and His Love Endures forever...

PSALM 100:5 NIV

He will cover you
with His pinions,
And under His wings
you may seek refuge;
His faithfulness is a shield.

PSALM 91:4 NASB

You could spend

your life

exploring God's love

and never reach

the end of it.

God cares about everything

in your life because He cares

so much about you.

Today

He wants to

fill your life

with joy and

free your heart

with love.

Make room
in your day
To show someone
God's love.

you WERE CALLED To freedom

GALATIANS 5:13 ESV

May 7

TO EVERYTHING

there is a season.

ECCLESIASTES 3:1 NKJV

August 25

May 6

God loves you so much because He knows you so well.

Friendship with God
is reserved for those
who reverence Him.

Your workmanship is

marvelous—

how well I know it.

PSALM 139:14 NLT

TAKE A MOMENT TODAY
TO THINK ABOUT SOMETHING
wonderful
GOD HAS DONE FOR YOU.

Who will
separate us
from the love
of Christ?

ROMANS 8:35 NASB

August 28

EVERY GOOD THING BEGINS WITH GOD.

No matter how deep the valley, *God's love is deeper.*

May 3

FAITH GROWS WITH EVERY STEP—AND IT TAKES A LIFETIME TO GET THERE.

August 29

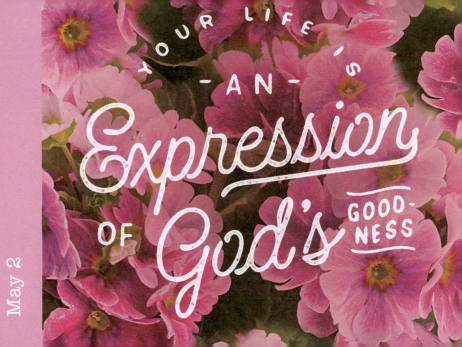

YOUR LIFE IS

-AN-

Expression

OF **God's** GOOD-NESS

May 2

A gracious woman
gets honor.

PROVERBS 11:16 NRSV

WE KNOW THAT ALL THINGS
WORK TOGETHER FOR GOOD
FOR THOSE WHO LOVE GOD,
WHO ARE CALLED
ACCORDING TO HIS PURPOSE.

ROMANS 8:28 NRSV

Don't hold back a kind word

or a loving deed—

God's heart

is written all over them.

They looked to Him and were

radiant,

and their faces
were not ashamed.

PSALM 34:5 NKJV

Rejoice in the Lord,
O you righteous.
Praise befits the upright.

PSALM 33:1 NRSV

When we live in
God's love for us,
we naturally

shine

with His beauty.

September 2

God makes all things beautiful.

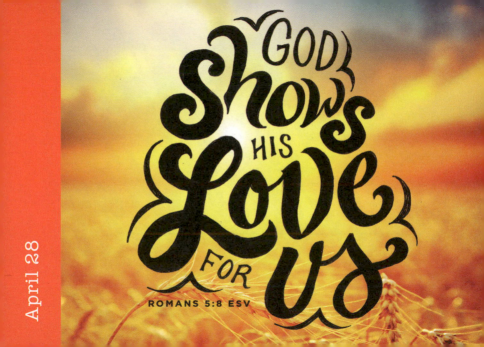

April 28

GOD SHOWS HIS LOVE FOR US

ROMANS 5:8 ESV

GOD HAS GIVEN YOU
something you can give
BACK TO THE WORLD—
in a way that
NO ONE ELSE CAN.

His love is
unconditional.

Every good thing I have comes from You.

PSALM 16:2 NLT

BE STILL, AND KNOW

THAT HIS LOVE FOR YOU

IS COMPLETE.

God's plan
for your life
is as special
as you are.

Be still,
AND KNOW
THAT I AM
God

PSALM 46:10 NKJV

April 25

Every time you praise God,
His heart leaps for joy!

September 6

In all the world,
there's no greater place of
rest and relaxation
than in the
love of God.

April 24

But thanks be to God,
who gives us the victory
through our Lord Jesus Christ.

I CORINTHIANS 15:57 NRSV

*For God alone
my soul waits.*

PSALM 62:1 NRSV

Find a place to be

alone with God...

and let it become

your favorite place to be.

We know how much God loves us, and we have put our trust in His love. God is love, and all who live in love live in God, and God lives in them.

1 JOHN 4:16 NLT

When you draw close to God,
God will draw close to you.

JAMES 4:8 TLB

September 9

You Are Wildly Loved.

April 21

You are
priceless
to God.

September 10

By this the love of God was manifested in us, that God has sent His only begotten Son into the world so that we might live through Him.

1 JOHN 4:9 NASB

Let us *consider* one another in order to stir up *love* and *good works.*

HEBREWS 10:24 NKJV

Do you realize
how much you mean
to God?

*Faith is having
the courage
to believe God
will do it
before we see it.*

God remains!
He is the strength of my heart;
He is mine forever!

PSALM 73:26 TLB

Now faith
is the assurance
of things hoped for,
the conviction
of things not seen.

HEBREWS 11:1 NASB

God's pursuit of your heart never stops.

THERE'S A CERTAIN LOVELINESS IN THE ONE WHO'S *in love with God.*

September 14

TO EVERYTHING THERE IS A

Season

A TIME FOR EVERY PURPOSE
UNDER HEAVEN...A TIME TO LOVE.

ECCLESIASTES 3:1, 8 NKJV

April 16

Love matters MOST.

God won't allow anything
to come to you
that hasn't first been screened
through His love.
Even challenges are
a time for seeking
His loving heart for you.

Submit therefore to GOD.

JAMES 4:7 NASB

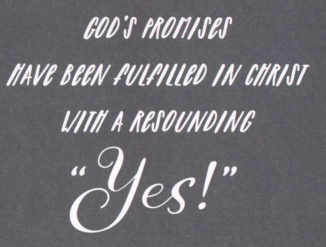

GOD'S PROMISES
HAVE BEEN FULFILLED IN CHRIST
WITH A RESOUNDING
"Yes!"

II CORINTHIANS 1:20 NLT

April 14

Only God can see everything.

ECCLESIASTES 8:17 TLB

September 17

THE FUTURE IS AS
Bright
AS THE
PROMISES OF GOD.
—WILLIAM CAREY

April 13

Friends

are an essential part
of God's goodness
to us.

Let us go right into the

presence of God

with sincere hearts

fully trusting Him.

HEBREWS 10:22 NLT

For we are
his workmanship,
created in Christ Jesus
for good works.

EPHESIANS 2:10 ESV

Your goodness

and unfailing kindness

shall be with me

all of my life.

PSALM 23:6 TLB

The Lord your God is in your midst...
He will exult over you with joy.

ZEPHANIAH 3:17 NASB

April 10

IT IS A

wonderful thing

TO BE ALIVE!

ECCLESIASTES 11:7 TLB

April 9

God delights in you!

God has a plan for you today— and it's good in every way.

April 8

God fills YOUR EVERY CHAPTER *with the plans* HE HAS WRITTEN *just for you.*

*Give generously, for your gifts
will return to you later.*

ECCLESIASTES 11:1 TLB

In Your book they all were written,
the days fashioned for me,
when as yet there were none of them.

PSALM 139:16 NIV

Rekindle the gift of God

that is within you.

II TIMOTHY 1:6 NRSV

Because Your lovingkindness
is better than life,
my lips will praise You.

PSALM 63:3 NASB

Be brave on the inside, where God does great things.

September 25

THE BEST LOVE IS
GOD'S love

April 5

The Lord longs to be gracious to you, and therefore He waits on high to have compassion on you.

ISAIAH 30:18 NASB

September 26

The human heart [has not] conceived, what God has prepared for those who love Him.

1 CORINTHIANS 2:9 NRSV

April 4

PRAISE HER FOR THE MANY FINE THINGS SHE DOES. THESE GOOD DEEDS OF HERS SHALL BRING HER HONOR.

PROVERBS 31:31 TLB

The best dreams
are the ones
God has in His heart
for you.

If you will stir up this inner power,

you will never be afraid.

II TIMOTHY 1:8 TLB

HEAR MY PRAYER,
O LORD....
IN YOUR FAITHFULNESS
ANSWER ME.

PSALM 143:1 NKJV

Lord,

MAKE ME ALL
YOU WANT ME TO BE!

September 29

BELIEVE IN THE *power* OF *prayer*, AND THE *faithfulness* OF OUR AMAZING, ALL-POWERFUL GOD.

SHE HAD A SPRING IN HER STEP, *God on her side,* AND A FEARLESS HEART *to face the day.*

September 30

YOU ARE

completely loved

BY THE

Creator

OF THE UNIVERSE.

March 31

Strive first for the kingdom of God

and His righteousness,

and all these things

will be given to you as well.

MATTHEW 6:33 NRSV

October 1

SEE HOW VERY MUCH
OUR FATHER LOVES US,
FOR HE CALLS US
His children.

I JOHN 3:1 NLT

PRESENT YOURSELVES TO GOD
AS BEING ALIVE FROM THE DEAD,
AND YOUR MEMBERS AS

*instruments
of righteousness*

TO GOD.

ROMANS 6:13 NKJV

Surely Your goodness
and unfailing love
will pursue me
all the days of my life.

PSALM 23:6 NLT

GLIMPSE THE BEAUTY
around you today—
IT'S NOTHING COMPARED TO
the beauty
WITHIN YOU.

October 3

ENJOY YOUR DAY

TO THE FULLEST and find

GOD'S GOODNESS

IN EVERY PART OF IT.

March 28

I CHOSE YOU,
AND APPOINTED YOU
THAT YOU WOULD GO
AND BEAR FRUIT.

JOHN 15:16 NASB

THE STEADFAST LOVE OF THE

Lord

NEVER CEASES!

LAMENTATIONS 3:22 NRSV

March 27

THE GRACEFUL *beauty of God* SHINES ON YOU.

Everywhere you go,
the love and presence
of God will go with you.

You're the joy
of God's heart
and the reason for
His song.

GOD LOVES YOU
LIKE CRAZY...
AND THAT WILL
NEVER CHANGE.

Every detail
of who you are
was designed
for the purposes
of God.

October 7

I have loved you
with an everlasting love.

JEREMIAH 31:3 NRSV

March 24

LET YOUR DREAMS *ignite your faith.*

October 8

Experience God's best in everything!

So do not worry about tomorrow,
for tomorrow will bring worries of its own.
Today's trouble is enough for today.

MATTHEW 6:34 NRSV

The Lord's blessing
is our greatest wealth.

PROVERBS 10:22 TLB

*Because of our faith,
He has brought us into this place
of highest privilege.*

ROMANS 5:2 TLB

You alone are my God;

my times are in Your hands.

PSALM 31:14 TLB

October 11

KIND WORDS
ARE LIKE
HONEY—
enjoyable
AND
healthful.

PROVERBS 16:24 TLB

Let your day rest in God's hands & enjoy where He takes you.

TODAY HAS

God loves you

WRITTEN ALL OVER IT!

March 19

Don't hide your light!
Let it shine for all.

MATTHEW 5:15-16 TLB

You
are precious to Me.
You are honored,
and I love you.

ISAIAH 43:4 NLT

Render service with enthusiasm,
as to the Lord and not to men
and women, knowing that
whatever good we do,
we will receive the same
again from the Lord.

EPHESIANS 6:7-8 NRSV

Yes, the Lord has done amazing things for us!

What joy!

PSALM 126:3 NLT

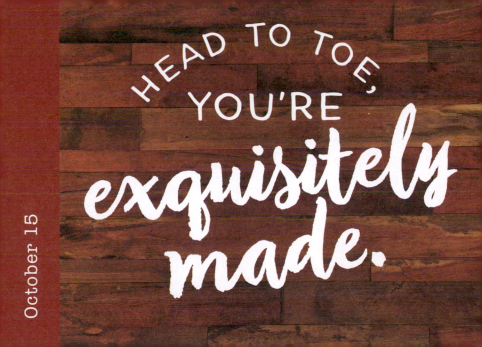

HEAD TO TOE, YOU'RE *exquisitely made.*

October 15

Celebrate
every great thing
the Lord is doing
in and through
your life.

March 16

SHINE YOUR GOD-GIVEN
light
ON THOSE AROUND YOU.

October 16

Yes, I will trust the promises of God.

PSALM 56:3 TLB

March 15

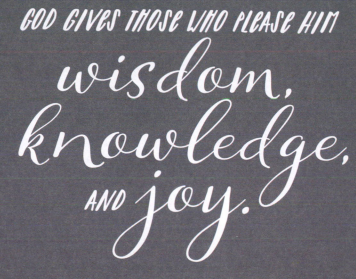

GOD GIVES THOSE WHO PLEASE HIM

wisdom,

knowledge,

AND *joy.*

ECCLESIASTES 2:26 TLB

October 17

If God
says it,
you can
TRUST it.

Put your heart into everything—
and see what God
will do through you.

The steadfast love
of the Lord is from
EVERLASTING TO EVERLASTING.

PSALM 103:17 NRSV

March 13

SO DO NOT WORRY
ABOUT TOMORROW,
FOR TOMORROW WILL BRING
WORRIES OF ITS OWN.
TODAY'S TROUBLE
IS ENOUGH FOR TODAY.

MATTHEW 6:34 NRSV

October 19

LOVE WILL NEVER END
BECAUSE OF GOD'S
never-ending love.

March 12

God puts each day together with a perfect eye for every detail.

Every good gift
and every perfect gift
is from above,
and comes down
from the Father.

JAMES 1:17 NKJV

Make Your face to shine
upon Your servant.

PSALM 31:16 NASB

*Every
good thing
is a gift
from God.*

Let the spirit of God
empower you to face
every challenge
with style and grace.

You are *precious*

in My sight,

and *honored,*

and I *love you.*

ISAIAH 43:4 NRSV

Jesus Christ is the same yesterday and today and forever.

HEBREWS 13:8 NASB

October 23

You are

valued

& loved

just because you're you!

You are delicately made and precious to your Maker.

October 24

I pray that you may...

know the love of Christ

that surpasses knowledge.

EPHESIANS 3:18–19 NRSV

March 7

Those who turn many to righteousness will glitter like stars forever.

DANIEL 12:3 TLB

October 25

Explore

the width, length,

height, and depth of

God's great love

for you.

Pursue peace with everyone.

HEBREWS 12:14 NRSV

The Lord will fulfill
His purpose for me;
your steadfast love, O Lord,
endures forever.

PSALM 138:8 NRSV

Put on *God's gentleness* and let it be a comfortable part of your life.

Celebrate
God's wonderful
plan for you.

March 4

October 28

Let everything He has made give praise to Him.

PSALM 148:5 TLB

March 3

TODAY YOU ARE SURROUNDED BY *God's love* + BLESSED BY HIS PEACE.

FACE YOUR DAY

WITH CONFIDENCE—

GOD IS WITH YOU!

The God of love and peace
will be with you.

II CORINTHIANS 13:11 NKJV

Remember the good.

Let go of the rest.

There are

NO LIMITS

to what

YOU AND GOD

can do

TOGETHER!

Sing aloud to God our strength; make a joyful shout.

PSALM 81:1 NKJV

October 31

WITH GOD
ALL things
are
possible!
Matthew 19:26
NKJV

Lord, let my life be a continual melody of *thankfulness* to you!

For God has not given us a spirit of fear, but of power and of love and of a sound mind.

II TIMOTHY 1:7 NKJV

Remind each other
of God's *goodness*
and be thankful.

EPHESIANS 5:4 TLB

You have the power of

God's love

within you and all
of heaven ahead of you.

IF WE'RE GOING TO BE
ENTHUSIASTIC ABOUT LIFE,
WE MUST BE PASSIONATE
ABOUT GOD.

[The Lord will] guide you
along the best pathway
for your life.

PSALM 32:8 TLB

Teach me to do Your will,
for You are my God.

PSALM 143:10 NRSV

LIVING BY FAITH IS LIFE'S GREATEST ADVENTURE.

There are some days when you just have to hang the **"Be Brave"** sign on your heart and dive in!

November 5

February 24

SHINE OUT
FOR ALL TO SEE.

MATTHEW 5:16 NLT

All who...trust in Him
are blessed
beyond expression.

PSALM 112:1 TLB

YOU BRING GOD'S BEAUTIFUL

LIGHT TO THE WORLD—

Let it shine!

There is

great gain in

godliness

combined

with contentment.

I TIMOTHY 6:6 NRSV

He has made everything beautiful in its time.

ECCLESIASTES 3:11 NKJV

Live. Laugh. Love. Pray. PRAISE. Every day!

Everything beautiful
BEGINS WITH GOD.

Wisdom is a fountain of life.

PROVERBS 16:22 TLB

November 9

I will praise You, for I am fearfully and wonderfully made.

PSALM 139:14 NKJV

There's a lot to be said

about choosing

happiness—

and it's best to remember...

it is a choice!

You are fearfully
and wonderfully made—
don't ever forget it!

Clouds are sometimes
the best way for our hearts
to learn to truly appreciate
the sunshine.

The reward for humility
and fear of the Lord
is riches and honor and life.

PROVERBS 22:4 NRSV

God loves you
no matter what.

THE ONLY *wealth* THAT MATTERS IS BEING RICH *in Christ*

Wisdom will come into your heart, and knowledge will be pleasant to your soul.

PROVERBS 2:10 NRSV

November 13

May the beloved of the Lord dwell in security by Him.

DEUTERONOMY 33:12 NASB

To grow in beauty and grace,

ask God to show you

the seeds you should plant

in the soil of your heart.

Wholly loved

with

holy love.

ON GOD RESTS
MY DELIVERANCE
AND MY HONOR;

MY MIGHTY ROCK,

MY REFUGE IS IN GOD.

PSALM 62:7 NRSV

God is
always
with me.

THERE IS **INCREDIBLE COMFORT** IN KNOWING GOD'S LOVE FOR YOU WILL NEVER CHANGE.

November 16

I am with you always

MATTHEW 28:20

-NKJV

November 17

Let the words of my mouth and the meditation of my heart be acceptable to you, O Lord, my rock and my redeemer.

PSALM 19:14 NRSV

February 12

He chose us in Him before the foundation of the world.

EPHESIANS 1:4 NKJV

There are a million reasons
to thank God
for being patient with us.

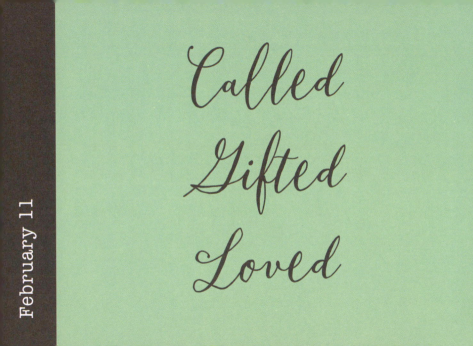

February 11

Called

Gifted

Loved

For the word of the Lord is upright,
and all His work is done in faithfulness.

PSALM 33:4 NRSV

The Lord...makes us
more and more like Him
as we are changed into
His glorious image.

II CORINTHIANS 3:18 NLT

November 20

MIRACLES HAPPEN
JOY STRENGTHENS
Love
CONQUERS ALL!

Who you are is a *beautiful reflection* of who God is.

God...*keeps faith*

forever.

PSALM 146:5–6 NRSV

O Lord,
You have searched
me and known
me.

PSALM 139:1 NASB

February 8

If God is for us,

who is against us?

ROMANS 8:31 NASB

God knew you first,

knows you best,

and loves you most.

The merciful man

does himself good.

PROVERBS 11:17 NASB

And you will know the truth,
and the truth
will make you free.

JOHN 8:32 NRSV

This day will bring opportunities to make God smile.

God's truth is my freedom.

Let us walk **in the light** of the Lord.

ISAIAH 2:5 NRSV

GOD IS

Love

1 JOHN 4:16
NKJV

God showed

His great love for us

by sending Christ.

ROMANS 5:8 TLB

Authentic love finds its source in God.

Life is all about

loving God

and loving others—

it really is

as simple as that.

Satisfy us in the morning with Your steadfast love, so that we may rejoice and be glad all our days.

PSALM 90:14 NRSV

May mercy and peace and love be multiplied to you.

JUDE 1:2 NASB

November 28

THE ONLY THING THAT TRULY SATISFIES IS THE *Love* OF CHRIST.

November 29

God is in control

Your gifts are beyond compare,
and with God, your dreams
are always within reach.

By His divine power,

God has given us

everything we need

for living a godly life.

II PETER 1:3 NLT

BEING FULL OF

joy and generosity,

EVERYONE KNEW HER HEART

BELONGED TO GOD.

Now to Him
who is able to do
far more abundantly
beyond all that
we ask or think,
according to the power
that works within us,
to Him be the glory.

EPHESIANS 3:20–21 NASB

HAPPY ARE THOSE

WHO TRUST IN

the Lord.

PROVERBS 16:20 NRSV

December 2

God takes
ordinary
and makes it
extraordinary!

Pray in the Spirit at all times.

EPHESIANS 6:18 NRSV

You deserve honesty from the heart.

PSALM 51:6 TLB

You can rest
in the arms
of your Savior.

She was

brave

on the inside,

where God does

beautiful

things.

Joy is the soul's celebration of everything God has done.

The love of God
has been poured out
in our hearts
by the Holy Spirit
who was given to us.

ROMANS 5:5 NKJV

January 25

GOD'S SON SHINES OUT
WITH GOD'S
glory.
HEBREWS 1:3 TLB

December 6

My heart,
God's love.

January 24

IN GOD'S EYES
YOU ARE *loved,*
AND YOU ARE

Lovely

THE ONLY THING
THAT COUNTS IS

faith

WORKING THROUGH

love.

GALATIANS 5:6 NRSV

Love one another,

EVEN AS I HAVE

LOVED YOU.

JOHN 13:34 NASB

EXPRESS YOUR FAITH

THROUGH LOVE.

Head up, shoulders back,
thoughts positive,
heart set on
the promises of God.

Let love be your highest goal!

I CORINTHIANS 14:1 NLT

All the paths
of the Lord
are mercy
and truth.

PSALM 25:10 NKJV

December 10

January 20

Love well

Refresh your soul
with hope
and let your spirit
be filled with

JOY!

December 11

My grace is sufficient for you, for **POWER** is perfected in weakness.

2 CORINTHIANS 12:9 NASB

For it is God who is at work in you.

PHILIPPIANS 2:13 NRSV

BROKEN BUT
beautiful.

The woman who loves wisdom is elegant beyond compare.

Clothe yourselves with

compassion, kindness,

humility, meekness

and *patience.*

COLOSSIANS 3:12 NRSV

If you search for good,
you
will find God's favor.

PROVERBS 11:27 TLB

December 14

Be the
real deal.

May God

who gives patience, steadiness,
and encouragement
help you live in complete

harmony.

ROMANS 15:5 TLB

December 15

January 15

TRUE BEAUTY IS ON THE INSIDE.

Whoever walks wisely
will be delivered.

PROVERBS 28:26 NKJV

A GENTLE AND QUIET SPIRIT... IS VERY PRECIOUS IN GOD'S SIGHT.

I PETER 3:4 NRSV

Being thankful is an easy way to fill our hearts with joy.

IN YOUR PRESENCE

IS FULLNESS OF

joy

PSALM 16:11 NKJV

God used
the infinite resources
of His goodness
to create you.

Live today with abundant joy,
knowing that you are
a child of God.

Miracles are God's way
of showing us
that if we believe,
all things are possible.

January 11

Perfectly imperfect...
and completely loved.

You are loved and cared for
every moment by the God
who holds the universe in His hands.

I have loved you, My people,

with an everlasting love.

With unfailing love

I have drawn you to Myself.

JEREMIAH 31:3 NLT

LORD, PUT MY FEET

on the path

YOU'VE CHOSEN FOR ME,

AND LET MY HEART

BE CONTENT.

My cup

overflows.

PSALM 23:5 NASB

KEEP TRAVELING
STEADILY ALONG HIS
pathway.

PSALM 37:34 TLB

December 22

You were made *to shine* from the inside out.

January 8

December 23

YOU ARE GOD'S
very best idea.

I am content with weaknesses,

insults, hardships, persecutions,

and calamities for the sake of Christ;

for whenever I am weak,

then I am strong.

II CORINTHIANS 12:10 NRSV

I will bless

The Lord

at all times;

His praise shall continually

be in my mouth.

PSALM 34:1 NKJV

Vulnerability isn't weakness;

it's strength.

January 6

WHOEVER KEEPS HIS WORD,
TRULY THE LOVE OF GOD
IS PERFECTED IN HIM.

I JOHN 2:5 NKJV

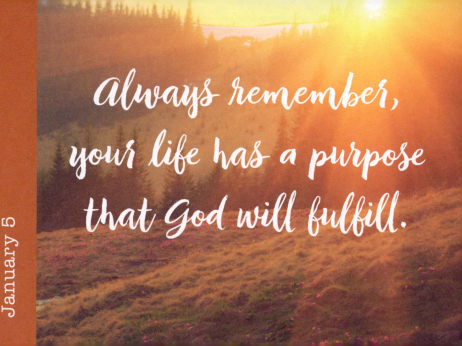

Always remember, your life has a purpose that God will fulfill.

There's no fear too big that His peace can't overcome.

Your loving-kindness, Lord, continues forever.

PSALM 138:8 TLB

Through [Him]
we have received grace...
for His name's sake.

ROMANS 1:5 NASB

THIS IS THE DAY
THE LORD HAS MADE;
WE WILL REJOICE
AND BE GLAD IN IT.

PSALM 118:24 NKJV

For from Him
and through Him
and to Him
are all things.

ROMANS 11:36 NRSV

LIVE TODAY WITH joy

January 2

GOD CELEBRATES YOU *every* day OF THE YEAR.

December 29

All glory to God.

EPHESIANS 3:20 NLT

January 1

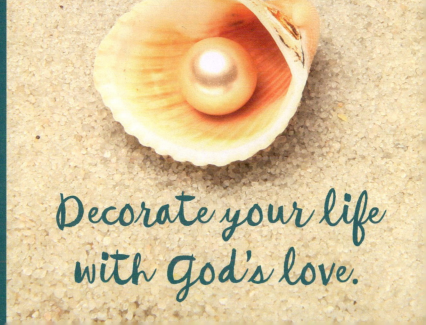

Decorate your life
with god's love.